A WINNING SKILLS BOOK

You Can Be a Star!

Joy Berry

Illustrated by Bartholomew

Joy Berry Enterprises

Copyright © Joy Berry, 2022
Originally Published 2013

All rights are reserved.

No part of this book can be duplicated or used without the prior written permission of the copyright owner, except for the use of brief quotations from the book.

For inquiries or permission requests contact the publisher.

Published by Joy Berry Enterprises
www.joyberryenterprises.com

You can be a star if you understand
- being famous or infamous,
- the six characteristics of stars,
- the two basic kinds of stars,
- some advantages and disadvantages of being a star,
- important information for stars, and
- the six steps to becoming a star.

BEING FAMOUS OR INFAMOUS

A **famous** person is one who has done something to capture the attention of many people and has become well known.

An **infamous** person is one who has become well known by doing something that is not socially acceptable.

BEING FAMOUS OR INFAMOUS

Some people think that a star is a person is either famous or infamous.

In reality, stars are never infamous. And, although some stars are famous, fame is not necessary to be a star.

SIX CHARACTERISTICS OF STARS

People who are stars have six basic characteristics.

Characteristic 1: A star is *recognized* by other people.

Others notice this person.

Characteristic 2: A star is *respected* by other people.

Others have positive thoughts about this person.

Characteristic 3: A star is *appreciated* by other people.

Others acknowledge and enjoy who the person is and what he or she does.

Characteristic 4: A star *receives special attention* from other people.

Others often make a special effort to treat the person well.

Characteristic 5: A star *can do one thing exceptionally well.*

The person excels in at least one area.

Characteristic 6: A star *affects other people in a positive way.*

The quality of other people's lives is enriched because of the person's influence and efforts.

TWO KINDS OF STARS

There are two basic kinds of stars.

Some stars are **little-known**. They are recognized by only a few people.

TWO KINDS OF STARS

Some stars are **well-known**. They are recognized by many people.

ADVANTAGES AND DISADVANTAGES OF BEING A STAR

As with everything, being a well-known star has advantages and disadvantages.

Here are some of the advantages:

A well-known star
- receives positive affirmation from many people that helps him or her develop a positive self-image and
- has access to many life-enriching opportunities.

A well-known star also
- attracts attention wherever he or she goes,
- does not have to make an effort to gain acceptance in new situations because he or she is already known, and
- is usually automatically accepted.

Here are some of the disadvantages of being a well-known star.

If a person is a well-known star, other people might
- be jealous of him or her,
- assume that he or she is conceited,
- feel inferior and thus avoid being around him or her, or
- be preoccupied with the star's being well known and ignore other good qualities about him or her.

A well-known star might also
- rely so much on being well-known that he or she fails to develop other, more important attributes and abilities.
- wonder whether he or she is liked only because of being well known and not for any other reason, and
- be fearful of not being liked if he or she ceases to be well known.

ADVANTAGES AND DISADVANTAGES OF BEING A STAR

Here are some other disadvantages of being a well-known star:

A well-known star might
- attract attention at a time when he or she does not want it and
- attract attention from people he or she does not want to associate with.

A well-known star might also find it extremely difficult to have any privacy.

This means that many people, including strangers, know a great deal about the person, including his or her imperfections, problems, and mistakes.

Being a little-known star also has advantages and disadvantages.

Here are some of the advantages.

A little-known star
- has only a few people to keep track of and to relate to and
- has only a few people making demands on his or her time, energy, and effort.

A little-known star
- can "blend into the crowd" whenever he or she wishes to do so and
- can have privacy whenever he or she wants it.

Here are some of the disadvantages of being a little-known star:

A little-known star
- must be content with the affirmation he or she receives from a limited number of people and
- has to create most of his or her own life-enriching opportunities.

A little-know star
- has to make an effort to be noticed by others and
- has to "prove" himself or herself to gain acceptance in new situations.

Even though there are disadvantages to being a star, almost everyone would like to be one.

Most people would like to be a star because they want to
- be recognized,
- be respected,
- be appreciated, and
- receive special attention.

Many people would also like to be able to
- do something well
- have a positive influence on other people's lives.

IMPORTANT INFORMATION FOR STARS

It is possible for you to become a star, but first you must understand some information every star needs to know.

There is a specific purpose for everything that exists in the natural universe. Everything contributes in some way to the world in which it is a part.

Every living organism is healthiest when it is fulfilling its purpose.

When an organism fulfills its purpose, it contributes to the world around it. In return it is valued and given what it needs to survive and grow.

This exchange is often called the balance of give and take.

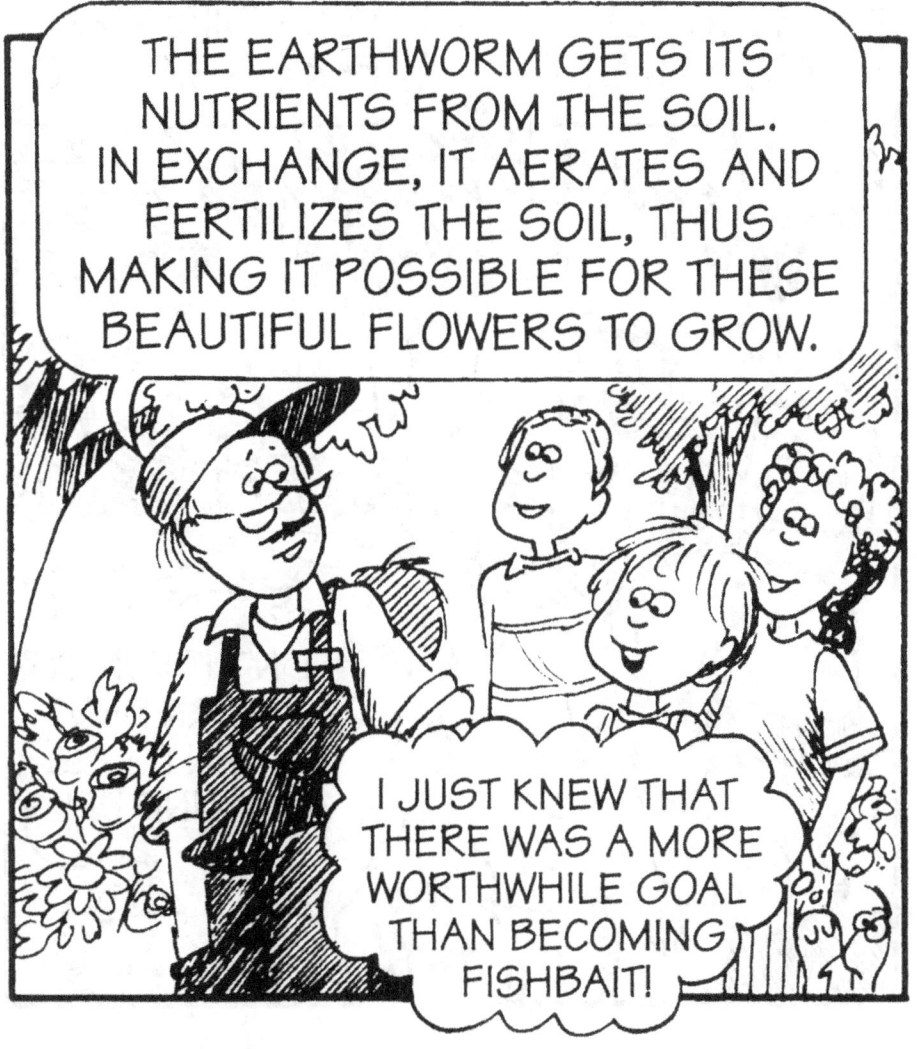

The balance of give and take is especially relevant to human beings.

People are healthiest and happiest when they are fulfilling their purpose.

When people fulfill their purpose, they contribute to the world around them. In return they are valued and given what they need to survive and grow.

IMPORTANT INFORMATION FOR STARS

The purpose each person is born to fulfill is one only that person can fulfill.

If for some reason a person fails to make his or her contribution, the world is deprived of it.

However, when a person makes his or her contribution, the world benefits from it, and the person automatically becomes a star.

When you contribute to the world by fulfilling the purpose for which you were born, you become a star.

Therefore, the key to becoming a star is finding your purpose in life and then fulfilling that purpose.

Discovering and fulfilling your purpose will be easier in life if you follow six steps.

Step 1: Determine what your gifts are.

A **skill** is the ability to do something. Skills are usually learned.

A **talent** is a skill that one has a natural ability to develop and do well.

A **gift** is a talent that one has a strong desire to use.

To determine what your gifts are, you need to decide what you
- do best,
- enjoy doing or enjoy the result of doing, and
- are most motivated to do.

It will help if you pay attention to what you
- do on your own without encouragement or prodding from other people,
- do in your free time when you can choose what to do, or
- are doing when you feel the happiest and most fulfilled.

Ask family members, friends, school counselors, or teachers to help determine what your gifts are if you have a difficult time doing so on your own.

Step 2: Determine how you can use your gifts to make a contribution.

Decide how you can use your gifts to enhance and enrich the world of which you are a part.

Decide how you can use your gifts to enhance and enrich the lives of the people around you.

Step 3: Develop your gifts.

Learn everything you can about your gifts, including
- where they can be used,
- how they can be used, and
- how to use them.

Develop skills associated with your gifts by practicing and using them whenever possible.

Step 4: Develop plans to use your gifts.

Determine how you can start using your gifts immediately.

Determine how you can use your gifts in the future.

Step 5: Put your gifts to use immediately.

Use your gifts whenever and wherever you can, including at
- home,
- school, and
- work.

If you find it difficult to use your gifts at home, school, or work, develop hobbies or seek out extracurricular activities that provide opportunities to use your gifts.

Step 6: Develop hobbies or a career that will allow you to use your gifts in the future.

Talk to adults with gifts similar to yours. Or, talk to school or career counselors. Find out what you need to do develop hobbies or a career that will utilize your gifts.

Follow the advice of the people you talk to. Seek out education, training, and experience necessary to develop your hobbies or career.

CONCLUSION

You might be the kind of star that contributes to the lives of a few people.

Or, you might be the kind of star who contributes to the lives of many people.

The *number* of people you influence is unimportant.

What is important is making a contribution to someone's life in addition to your own.

Therefore, the focus needs to be on what you can give rather than on what you can receive out of life.

If you concentrate on what you can give, you will make a contribution to the world of which you are a part, and this will make you a star.